UNITY

GOD'S PERFECT PLAN FOR JOYFUL LIVING

GWEN CAMPBELL

John 17:21

"That they all may be one, as You, Father, are in Me,
and I in You; that they also may be one in Us, that the world
may believe that You sent Me."

xulon
PRESS

DEDICATION

I dedicate this book to my Heavenly Father, who placed the desire in my heart to write it to encourage His people. Our Father wants us to follow the heart of His dear Son, whose prayer was for us to be unified. The Father, Son, and the Holy Spirit know the blessings of unity; as they are three, but they operate as one. As I dedicate this book to Him, my only hope is that it will be pleasing to Him and will bring about the results that He desire for His people; the Body of Christ.

I also want to dedicate this book to a young man I met at a Juvenile Detention Center, who I will call "Hunter." I was there to bless him, but as it turned out; he really blessed me. At the age of 15, this young man spoke to my heart about unity amongst people of all races and cultures. I told him this was the heartbeat of God and shared scripture with him regarding unity. His eyes lit up when we read the scriptures from John 17. It was then that I shared this book with him. He looked at me and said "Will you put me in your book? And I replied "Sure I will." So this book is also dedicated to Hunter, who touched my life on the subject of unity.

Contents

FOREWORD

I count it an honor to write the foreword to this descriptive work of UNITY.

As I sat down and read this book, it was like taking a pictorial journey through the Bible from the beginning, to the finality, to make this a team effort. Apostle Gwen has broken down the Bible from the creation to the cross, to the very simple promises.

This book is a pleasant easy read that will provoke you to learn how to accomplish the goal of Unity. She explains so uniquely for all to understand, that the "Sound of a Symphony" has many instruments {as we are} making one sound! I would recommend this reading as a tool to move all individuals into a personal journey of UNITY.

Apostle Gwen is a wonderful steadfast woman of God who is purposed to see others knowing the Lord our Savior in a very special way. Her heart yearns to see us as the Body of Christ working in complete manifestation of the word of God! This, as she has described, will only happen if we can come together on one accord.

This book has ignited my spirit to make sure in all that I am doing, is done in a spirit of unity so others will come along and feel the joy of the Lord, through such a love of one.

Thank you, Apostle, for stirring the Body of Christ in a unique truthful way....It started from creation and covers every area of our lives.

Apostle Shirley R. Brown,
Senior Leader of Destiny International Ministries
Founder of NNKA {No Nonsense Kingdom Alliance}

PREFACE

One of Jesus' greatest desires was for His people, the Body of Christ to become unified as one. This was the heart-cry of His prayer, in John 17, when He prayed to His Father that we all may be one as He and the Father are one.

Unity is being in harmony, in one accord, continuity without deviation. It is the power of oneness; being of one mind.

It is as the sound of a symphony. Although there are many instruments involved in a symphony; the sound is as one. There are also many members in the Body of Christ and we, too, are to function as one. Our voice should be as one, and our mind should be as one mind (the mind of Christ).

Unity is necessary in every area of life, if we are to be successful and live stressed free lives. You will find that it is absolutely necessary in the church; in our marriages, our families, and "yes", even in the workplace. Oh how wonderful it would be if unity was found in our government as well.

In the Book of Acts, we find one of the greatest gifts ever given, other than salvation. This gift is the baptism of the Holy Spirit. The Holy Spirit came in all of His fullness, only after they had prayed and were in one accord.

It is my prayer that this book will help you to understand the importance of unity, and that you will seek after it with all your heart, to bring you into the place where Jesus Christ prayed you would be. For it is there, you will be blessed beyond measure.

All scripture quotes are taken from the New King James Version of the Bible.

Chapter 1

Everybody is not like Me

*I*n the world we live in, we may often think that everything would be alright if everyone was just like us. What a wonderful world it would be.

We think we wouldn't have any problems; at all, because we would all think alike. We would all want to do the exact same things. We probably would all dress alike, eat the same kinds of food, go to the same places, work the same kinds of jobs, and drive the same cars. As a matter of fact, all the cars would look alike.

How boring would that be? It's also beginning to sound a little scary, isn't it? This may sound somewhat extreme, but this is exactly what life would be if we were all alike. In my estimation, this would soon turn into a much bigger problem than we could ever imagine. I believe life would become so undesirable that it could cause severe emotional problems.

As I said, I know this sounds a little extreme, but I really want you to think about this. There have been times when I have said, "if he (or she) was more like me, (especially my husband), then we wouldn't have any problems." As I have been awakened into reality; I know now that that is far from the truth. It is not the way God has planned us. He made us all different because He had a unique purpose in mind for each of us.

Imagine how mundane life would be if we were all the same. What would it look like if we all looked the same and talked the same with the same voice? The world would be extremely boring and it would not be somewhere we would want to be for very long. Nevertheless, so many of us often think, as I did at one time, that if he or she thought like me, we wouldn't have a problem. If he or she had the same idea as I have, everything would be okay.

We feel that way because we think we are right, and everybody else just needs to see things our way. Have you ever been guilty of thinking that way? There is a better way, and we can look to God's design for us. God made us each differently, because to complete our unique purpose; He knew we needed diversity.

Our God, who is awesome in every way, created us with differences. When He created male and female; He created them to be different. God has a plan for mankind; and the animals, plants and trees to all be different, for the sake of reproduction. God is much more brilliant than we are, and He knew that two of the same kind could not reproduce.

God created us all different because He wanted a variety of people. Amazingly, no two people are the same. No two people have the same DNA. Of all the seven billion people in the world, we are all different. Our God is truly amazing, and He knows what's best for us.

Some of you reading this book may be an identical twin, or know someone who is. And it's very interesting that identical twins have almost identical DNA and can still develop different personalities. Some twins even end up living totally different lives. Despite having the same genetic makeup; identical twins have their own distinctive personalities. For example, one may be very interested in playing basketball and enjoying other sports, while the other may have no interest in sports, at all, but is a lover of music and song writing. Just how their individuality emerges has remained a bit of a mystery.

There was a very interesting set of twins in the Bible, recorded in Genesis 25: 21-27. Their names were Jacob and Esau. They were the twin sons of Isaac and Rebekah. They came out of the womb fighting to see who would be first. The Bible doesn't say whether they were identical twins or not, but they did lead totally different lives, and it was all a part of God's plan.

Our God so appreciates variety that He created different races of people. He filled the earth with all kinds of mammals, insects, and reptiles, as well as species of trees and plants that are all uniquely different. Our universe is so diverse that it's almost mind boggling, including the planets in our solar system that are all different; none of them seem the same. They all have their unique purpose. Our Milky Way Galaxy is one of billions of systems, each including stars, nebulae, star clusters, globular clusters and interstellar matter that make up our amazing, awesome universe.

Even the clouds and the stars are all different shapes and sizes. No one could put together something as beautiful, with such magnitude as the universe, but our God! There is a lot more that could be said about the beauty and diversity of God's creation but hopefully, I've given you enough to cause you to appreciate the beauty and purpose of us not being alike, but all being different. It is all a part of God's plan and when we can grasp a hold of God's design and plan for us; it will make us even more beautiful, when we bring them together in harmony.

In **Genesis 1: 20-28**, we find these words:

"Then God said, "Let the waters abound with an abundance of living creatures, and let birds fly above the earth across the face of the firmament of the heavens." So God created great sea creatures and every living thing that moves, with which the waters abounded, according to their kind, and every winged bird according to its kind. And God saw that it was good. And God blessed them, saying, "Be fruitful and multiply, and fill the waters in the seas, and let birds multiply on the earth." So the evening and the morning were the fifth day. Then God said, "Let the earth bring forth the living creature according to its kind: cattle and creeping thing and beast of the earth, each according to its kind" and it was so. And God made the beast of the earth according to its kind, cattle according to its kind, and everything that creeps on the earth according to its kind. And God saw that it was good. Then God said, "Let Us make man in Our image, according to our likeness; let them have dominion over the fish of the sea, over the birds of the air, and over the cattle, over all the earth and over every creeping thing that creeps on the earth." So God created man in His own image; in the image of God He created him; male and female He created them. Then God blessed them and God said to them, "Be fruitful and multiply; fill the earth and subdue it; have dominion over the fish of the sea, over the birds of the air, and over every living thing that moves on the earth."

God is an intentional God, and He intentionally created everything different so all could reproduce, multiply, and fill the earth. He created diversity in His creation so the Earth would continue to perpetually replenish, and create the variety of living creatures He had in the imagery of His mind before time began.

I once heard a person, closely related to me, say "I don't need anybody; I can make it all by myself." That is so not true. Even if you think you don't need anyone, you do need me and I need you. We need each other. This was God's intention for building relationships. Our God is really big on relationships. He created us to be interdependent and not independent. This doesn't mean that we will always agree with each other, but it does mean we will always be free to agreeably disagree.

God wants to give us the opportunity to bring our differences together and work through them, so that we can find those things we agree on and build on them to advance His Kingdom.

When we disagree on things and do it agreeably, in the spirit of love; we are still operating in unity.

To have unity and harmony, there must be diversity. If we were all the same; looked alike, talked alike and did everything alike, there would be no diversity, and life would be boring. It is in diversity that we can have a wide ranged variety of people coming together to create a harmony as the sound of a symphony. This is unity at its best.

Once we accept the fact that everyone else is not like us and they don't have to be like us, neither should they be; it is then that we must accept them for who they are. We have to respect and accept their gifts and talents that God has given them. We can then combine our gifts and talents and create something beautiful for the Kingdom of God in the spirit of unity.

Chapter 2

I Need Your Gift, You Need My Gift

*S*piritual gifts are a good example of diversity in unity. The Apostle Paul wrote the following in **I Corinthians 12: 1, 4-11**:

"Now concerning spiritual gifts, brethren, I do not want you to be ignorant. There are diversities of gifts, but the same Spirit. There are differences of ministries, but the same Lord. And there are diversities of activities, but it is the same God who works all in all. But the manifestation of the Spirit is given to each one for the profit of all. For to one is given the word of wisdom through the Spirit, to another the word of knowledge through the same Spirit, to another the working of miracles, to another prophecy, to another discerning of spirits, to another different kinds of tongues, to another the interpretation of tongues. But one and the same Spirit works all these things, distributing to each one individually as He wills."

According to these scriptures, we don't all have the same gifts, but we need all our gifts to be operative in the Body of Christ today. It's the Holy Spirit who distributes these gifts to whom He wills. Each one of us is unique as members of the Body, and each one of us is needed in the Body. All members are dependent upon the Body, and no member can function properly apart from the Body.

Unity is not found in the possession of one common gift, but rather in all the gifts operating under the power and guidance of the Holy Spirit; who is the source of all the gifts. There are also different ministries in the Body, but the commonality or unity, in that is whatever we do is done for the same Lord, serving others and not ourselves.

It is the same God who empowers each one of us to function in our gift. If one gift seems more spectacular or powerful than another, it is not because of any superiority in the person possessing the gift. It is the anointing and power of God operating through the person. There is not a believer who has not received a gift to function in. The Holy Spirit manifests Himself in the life of each believer by imparting some gift for the profit of the entire Body. The gifts are given in order for us to help each other. That's why I need your gift, and you need my gift.

I remember my earlier years as a Christian, wanting to be like others and wanting to do things like they did. As a result; I was coveting their gifts, but did not know it at the time. It was only when I began to grow in my Christian walk that I realized what I was doing. Once the discovery was made; I immediately repented and asked God for His forgiveness.

God does not want us to covet another's gift, but He wants us to be the unique person He has ordained us to be, and operate in the gift or gifts He has given us through His Holy Spirit. Unity is not being the same; it's being different yet coming together, bringing all the different parts and pieces working together. **Isaiah 65:8a** "Thus says the Lord: "As the new wine is found in the cluster." This speaks to me, in that the new wine is not found in just one grape, but in the cluster. You can get a lot more juice out of a cluster of grapes than you can just one.

There are no inferior parts in the Body of Christ. God made us to complement each other since the beginning of creation. Adam and Eve were meant to complement each other. Adam was Eve's protector, and Eve was his helper. Their gifts, so to speak, complemented each other. They were created for each other, and so was each one of us. It is time that we be joined together in heart, faith and unity.

In order to bring our gifts together, we must bring our hearts together. It is then that we will have but one purpose, and with our mouth, we will, in essence, say the same thing. When you've heard one of us, you should have heard all of us. It is then that we will walk in **I Corinthians 10:31b** "Whatever you do, do all to the glory of God."

A prime example of bringing our gifts and our hearts together is found in a ministry I work with called Agape Ambassadors, Inc. This is a prison ministry that works with juveniles in Juvenile

Detention Centers. We have team members from all walks of life, different ages, different denominations and different gifts. We are all there for one purpose, and that is to bring hope and the love of Jesus to the teenagers. Therefore, there is never any competition amongst us, for we blend our gifts and hearts together for one purpose.

When we bring our gifts together, it is as if a great orchestra is gathering. The different instruments (gifts) are there to express their own individuality. Under the baton of The Great Conductor, the orchestra is capable of blending different sounds to produce the greatest symphonies. This is what our gifts do when we blend them together, they produce the greatest ministries to the Body of Christ that's ever needed. This will be found wherever believers focus together on the Lord, expressing their common commitment to Him and to each other. **Romans 12: 10** "Be kindly affectionate to one another with brotherly love, in honor giving preference to one another."

Chapter 3

Forming One New Man

In **Ephesians 4:11-13**, we find these words:

"And He Himself gave some to be apostles, some prophets, some evangelists, and some pastors and teachers, for the equipping of the saints for the work of the ministry, for the edifying of the body of Christ, till we all come to the unity of the faith and of the knowledge of the Son of God, to a perfect man, to the measure of the stature of the fullness of Christ." In **Galatians 3:28** the Bible further states that "There is neither Jew nor Greek, there is neither slave nor free, there is neither male nor female; for you are all one in Christ Jesus."

The purpose for God in giving gifts to men was for the equipping of the saints for the work of the ministry to build up the body of Christ. Consequently, the gifts equip the saints. The saints then serve and the body is built up. This includes every form of spiritual service; therefore every believer should be in some type of ministry.

In essence; we don't come to church just to hear the word, but to receive it and then go out and do it by allowing the word to become a part of our very lives. We are to tell others about the good news of the gospel so their lives will be changed so they, too, can witness to others. **Ephesians 4: 13** "Till we all come to the unity of the faith and of the knowledge of the Son of God, to a perfect man, to the measure of the stature of the fullness of Christ."

Under the law, there was a distinction between Jew and Gentile, slave and free, male and female. We find in Christ Jesus, all these differences disappear, in as far as our acceptance with God. God is a God of unity, a Jew is not preferred over a Gentile, a free man is not more favored than a slave, nor is a man more privileged than a woman. We are all on the same level because we are all one in Christ. There is no difference in the Spirit. In the Spirit, God sees us as one; the one new man that's formed through Jesus Christ. In the Spirit, we are all called sons of God.

In **Galatians 4: 5-6**, it says "To redeem those who were under the law, that we might receive the adoption as sons. And because you are sons, God has sent forth the Spirit of His Son into your hearts crying out, Abba, Father! How awesome is that? This means that all races, classes and sexes are one in Christ and equal in rights and privileges regarding the ministry of the gospel. The gulf between Jews and Gentiles, masters and slaves, male and female has been bridged by Christ and the good news of His great gospel. All Christians are, now, one in unity in rights and in priv-ileges as the Father, the Son and the Holy Spirit are one in unity.

Praise God for the one new man that's been formed. Even though the one new man has been formed in the Spirit; we must do something about it in the natural. We have to desire the unity of "one new man" through Jesus Christ, just as He prayed in John 17. We have to come out of our old mindsets of who we think we are and step into the new of who Jesus says we are. We have to be willing to receive all that Jesus came to give us, beginning with salvation as our first step to becoming this one new man.

Jesus prayed fervently and sincerely in **John 17**, for this to happen. Jesus knew the importance of us becoming one, because He, His Father and the Holy Spirit are one. He has known since before the foundations of the world, the importance of being one.

In Acts 2, when the Day of Pentecost had fully come, they were all with one accord (unity) in one place. Suddenly there came a sound from heaven, as a rushing mighty wind, and it filled the whole house where they were sitting. They were all filled with the Holy Spirit and began to speak with other tongues, as the Spirit gave them utterance.

This is what can happen when we get on one accord! It is then that we will begin to see some "suddenlies" in our churches and in our prayer meetings. When we're in one accord, the Spirit of the Lord will move. For it is in unity that God commands the bless-ings (**Psalm 133**), which I will talk more about later in the book.

Matthew 18:19 says "Again I say to you that if two of you agree on earth concerning anything that they ask, it will done for them by My Father in heaven." I like to summarize this scripture by saying "If we agree, anything can happen."

It is very important to realize that we have to want the one new man to be formed in our churches and in our Christian circles. If we do not desire it and be willing to work at it, and allow nothing to stop us; it will not come forth. In as much as Jesus wants it for us, He will not force it on us. We have to desire it as well.

When we began to come together with one mindset, in one accord, we will begin to see the miraculous things of God happening right in our midst. We will begin to see the lame walk, the deaf hear, and the blind see. We will begin to see the miraculous power of God moving among us. We will do the greater works that Jesus said we could do; if we believe.

(See more on "Forming One New Man in Chapter 4)

Chapter 4

The Cross Made Us One

The cross exhibits the wisdom and eternal purpose of God, which He accomplished through His Son, Jesus Christ. Before the world was made, God knew Satan would fall and man would follow him in sin. Therefore, He had already prepared a counterstrategy that would bring us back into oneness through the cross. This strategy has been worked out in the incarnation, death, resurrection, ascension, and glorification of Christ. The whole plan was centered in Christ and has been realized through Him, enabling God to save both Jews and Gentiles; making them members of the Body of Christ into the one new man.

In our understanding of the meaning of the cross; we realize this was an act by which God restored the relationship of harmony and unity between Himself and us. Having said that, let's look at the word "atonement." If we divide it into three syllables, it would read "at-one-ment." Through God's atoning grace and forgiveness, we were reinstated to a relationship of at-one-ment with God through the sacrificial death of His Son on the cross. God and man were brought back into a relationship in which they are one.

In Hebrew, the word for atonement is "kippur" and it means "covering." The Day of Atonement was a day of offering sacrifices to provide covering for the sins of the people of the Old Testament; but only for one year. The next year, at the same time, they had to again offer sacrifices to cover their sins. It provided no permanent solution, only a temporary covering. In the New Testament; the Atonement is totally different. When Jesus came and offered Himself as a sacrifice on the cross; He abolished sin once and for all. In **John 1:29b,** the Apostle John said "Behold! The Lamb of God who takes away the sin of the world!"

Imagine that! Jesus took away the sins of the whole world! For that reason; for those who have accepted His sacrifice, there remains no further sacrifice for sins. Now, our old man (the person we used to be before we accepted Jesus) has died in Jesus, and our new man (the person we are once we have accepted Jesus) is alive in us.

Romans 6:5-8:

"For if we have been <u>united together</u> in the likeness of His death, certainly we also shall be in the likeness of His resurrection, knowing this, that our old man was crucified with Him, that the body of sin might be done away with, that we should no longer be slaves of sin. For he who has died has been freed from sin. Now if we died with Christ, we believe that we shall also live with Him."

This means living with Him as the new man. The one who has been reconciled to God.

As we continue to refer to Jesus' death on the cross, according to the above scriptures in Romans 6; we see that our old man was crucified with Him. This is a biblical, historical fact; although the crucifixion of your old man with Christ cannot work in your life until you know and believe it. Anyone in whom the old man has not been dealt with is still a slave of sin; Romans 6 makes this very clear. The old man who has died with Christ has been freed from sin and reconciled to God, at one with Him.

Someone may be asking the question "How does this take place?" It takes place when we put our faith in what Jesus did for us, on the cross. When we put our faith in the finished work of Calvary, and accept the Lord, Jesus Christ as our Savior; our old man (the rebel) was executed.

Here is another way of looking at it. We have to change from the old to the new, and the only way to change a person is to make him or her a new creation; meaning we've got to be born again by the Spirit. We were born once physically, and our second birth is spiritual, through repentance and acceptance the Lord Jesus Christ as our Savior. God does not patch up or reform the old man. He does not educate him; He puts him to death. In his place, comes forth the new creation that is the product of God's truth. **2 Corinthians 5:17** says "If anyone is in Christ, he is a new creation; old things have passed away; behold, all things have become new."

God's purpose in all of this was not just for you and me, as Gentiles, to be reconciled to Him. It was for all mankind; the Jew first. **Ephesians 2:11-18:**

"Therefore remember that you, once Gentiles in the flesh – who are called Uncircumcised (Gentiles did not have the surgical mark in their flesh) by what is called the Circumcision (It identified the Jews as God's chosen people) made in the flesh by hands – that at that time you were without Christ, being aliens from the commonwealth of Israel and strangers from the covenants of promise, having no hope and without God in the world. But now in Christ Jesus you who once were far off have been brought near by the blood of Christ. For He Himself is our peace, who has made both one, and has broken down the middle wall of separation, having abolished in His flesh the enmity, that is, the law of commandments contained in ordinances, so as to create in Himself one new man from the two, thus making peace, and that He might reconcile them both to God in one body through the cross, thereby putting to death the enmity. And He came and preached peace to you who were afar off and to those who were near. For through Him we both have access by one Spirit to the Father."

Praise God! He has made us one with Him, both Jew and Gentile through the finish work of Calvary. The cross has truly made us one.

Chapter 5

Unity in the Church

The Greek word for church is ekklesia. This word is used 115 times in the New Testament, mostly in the book of Acts. At least 92 times, this word refers to a local congregation, or a local assembly of believers. Some of us, before coming to the understanding of who the church is, thought it was the church building. There's nothing wrong when passing by a place of worship, to say "Oh, there's a church." It's okay to call the building a church, as long as we have the understanding that it's only a <u>place</u> of worship.

We have to be clear on who the church really is as the ekklesia. The ekklesia refers to all those who follow Christ. The ekklesia is not a part of a cult, nor is it a part of the occult. It's a local assembly of believers as well as the redeemed of all ages who follow Jesus Christ as Savior and Lord.

The church at large is known as the Body of Christ and it did not begin until the day of Pentecost, after the ascension of Jesus. Before Jesus ascended, he said to His disciples in **Luke 24: 49-53**

"Behold, I send the Promise of My Father upon you; but tarry in the city of Jerusalem until you are endured with power from on high. And He began to lead them out as far as Bethany, and He lifted up His hands and blessed them. Now it came to pass, while He blessed them, that He was parted from them and carried up into heaven. And they worshiped Him, and returned to Jerusalem with great joy, and were continually in the temple praising and blessing God. Amen."

Acts 2: 1-4: "When the Day of Pentecost had fully come, they were all with one accord in one place. And suddenly there came a sound from heaven, as of a rushing mighty wind and it filled the whole house where they were sitting. Then there appeared to them divided tongues, as of fire, and one sat upon each one of them. And they were all filled with the Holy Spirit and began to speak with other tongues, as the Spirit gave them utterance."

As you can clearly see from the scriptures in Luke and Acts, the church was born in power and in UNITY, for they were all in one accord. It was NOT as some of our churches appear to be today, in weakness with no power. It did not have a form of godliness, denying the power thereof. No, the early church, in Acts, was born in power. So much so, that when Peter stood up, with the other 11 Apostles, to preach, the people around them were amazed and thought they were drunk. But Peter said in **Acts 2: 15-16:**

"For these are not drunk, as you suppose, since it is only the third hour of the day. But this is what was spoken by the prophet Joel." **Acts 2: 38-39:** "Then Peter said to them, 'Repent, and let every one of you be baptized in the name of Jesus Christ for the remission of sins; and you shall receive the gift of the Holy Spirit. For the promise is to you and your children, and to all who are afar off, as many as our God will call.' **Acts 2: 42-44:** "And they continued steadfastly in the Apostles' doctrine and fellowship, in the breaking of bread and in prayers. Then fear came upon every soul, and many wonders and signs were done through the apostles. Now all who believe were together, and had all things in common.

What a beautiful picture of unity these scriptures paint! For it is in unity that miracles, signs and wonders are performed. When we come into the power of agreement and unity, anything can happen. **Matthew 18:19** says; "Again I say to you that if two of you agree on earth concerning anything that they ask, it will be done for them by my Father in heaven."

When the church of the Living God is in unity, the devil has NO power over them. For Jesus said in **Luke 10:19;** "Behold I give you the authority to trample on serpents and scorpions, and over ALL the power of the enemy, and nothing shall by any means hurt you." This is a word Jesus gave to the seventy disciples as He sent them out to preach the kingdom of God. This word is also for His ekklesia, the church, today.

Unity in the Body of Christ is both, men and women working together in harmony to achieve a common goal for a common cause. Even though we are not all doing the same job, and we are not all working at the same pace; we are all are working together to advance the kingdom of God in the earth. It also means giving the people the right to sing their part and sound their own note, yet making sure they are in harmony with the Great Orchestrator, and the vision of the body.

God doesn't do math the way we do it. The Bible says in **Leviticus 26:8-9;** "Five of you shall chase a hundred, and a hundred of you shall put ten thousand to flight; your enemies shall fall by the sword before you. For I will look on you favorably and make you fruitful, multiply you and confirm My covenant with you." This is what happens when the church, the Body of Christ is working together in unity.

We were not created to ever be alone. That's why God gave Adam a helper suitable for him. We all need someone in our lives. Even if you are a single person, you still need someone in your life; such as a prayer partner. You will need someone to come in agreement with, to advance God's kingdom in the earth. **Ecclesiastes 4: 9-10;** "Two are better than one, because they have a good reward for their labor. For if they fall, one will lift up his companion. But woe to him who is alone when he falls, for he has no one to help him up."

God is looking for people in His church, who are willing to crucify their own agendas; who are not worried about anything else but finding out what He wants them to do. In that alone, we would be astonished at the power He would release to the church. Imagine how wonderful it is when God finds five people in church, who are banning together in unity, putting 100 demonic forces to flight!

And even more awesome is to find 100 people banning together putting 10,000 demonic forces to flight! In some scriptures, the numbers are even greater for the amount of demonic forces that could be put to flight. This is the kind of power God would release, to us, to dispel demonic powers, which would be in direct proportion to the amount of unity we were willing to walk in.

Most importantly, the church must get in agreement with heaven. We can agree with each other about a lot of things, but in order to see the power of God move, we have to be in alignment with God's word.

The prayer Jesus prayed in John 17 was for the church, the Body of Christ, to be one, just as He and the Father are one. **John 17:21** "That they ALL may be one, as You, Father, are in Me, and I in You; that they also may be one in Us, that the world may believe that You sent Me." Jesus was praying that all believers might be one, because this is the unity that would make the world see Christ in Christians, as the Father was seen in Christ. This is the unity that would cause sinners to want to come to Christ.

Ephesians 4: 3-6; "Endeavoring to keep the unity of the Spirit in the bond of peace. There is one body and one Spirit, just as you were called in one hope of your calling; one Lord, one faith, one baptism; one God and Father of all, who is above all, and through all, and in you all."

The unity of the church is the work of the Holy Spirit. The Holy Spirit knits believers together. The Spirit breaks down walls of division, denominational barriers and racial barriers. When believers in EVERY Christian setting yield to the leading of the

Holy Spirit and allow Him to lead, guide and direct them; we will see unity in the church. However, I don't believe we will see the <u>fullness</u> of unity until we are dwelling in the presence of the Lord forever.

> **I Corinthians 13:12** "For now we see in a mirror, dimly, but then face to face. Now I know in part, but then I
>
> shall know just as I also am known."

Chapter 6

The Blessing of God
Released in Unity

Psalm 133: "Behold, how good and how pleasant it is for brethren to dwell together in unity! It is like the precious oil upon the head, running down on the beard, the beard of Aaron, running down on the edge of his garments. It is like the dew of Hermon descending upon the mountains of Zion; for there the Lord commanded the blessing – life forevermore."

This Psalm has stood out to me, for many years, because the Lord put it in my heart years ago to teach His Body about the importance of unity. With the pastor's permission, I even had it printed, framed and hung in the vestibule of the church I was attending. I wanted everyone who entered its doors to know that the church was a church that was trying to operate in the unity of the Spirit of God. Even if we weren't there yet, it was certainly the goal that we were working toward.

Psalm 133 is very short in terms of the number of words it contains, but it is EXTREMELY important in the quality of its words. The psalmist, David, has four main points in the Psalm. The first point is that it is **good** and **pleasant** for brethren to dwell together in unity! Second, it is **precious** and it is **fragrant.** Third, it is **refreshing.** Finally, it is the sure **guarantee** of God's blessing.

On things that are of value, based on the word of God and heaven's view of things, there must be agreement. On subordinate matters there is freedom for differing of opinions, because we are all different, but that does not prevent our working together. Even on the subordinate matters, at some point; you may need to agree. All members of the human body are different, but as they operate in obedience to the Head; there is glorious unity! And in all things the spirit of love MUST be in operation.

Unity carries a sweet smelling fragrance wherever it is in operation. **(Psalm 133:2)** It's like the anointing oil that was poured on Aaron's head, and ran down his beard and down to the edge of his robe. The pleasing fragrance was not only enjoyed by the priest, but by everyone in the area. The precious anointing oil gives a picture of the Holy Spirit, descending as a sweet-smelling fragrance on the people of God when they are working together in unity.

Unity is refreshing like the morning dew. **(Psalm 133:3a)** It is like the dew of Hermon, descending upon the mountains of Zion. The dew of Hermon is the source of cool, invigorating moisture descending down on other mountains. It's like the Holy Spirit carrying the refreshment of the unity of the brethren to reach others. This is what happens when we walk in fellowship with God and with one another.

The final point in the Psalm is that the Lord commands the blessing where believers are operating in the spirit of unity. As mentioned in Chapter five; The Day of Pentecost is a good example of unity and blessings upon believers. The disciples were united in prayer, waiting for the promise of the Holy Spirit, when suddenly the Spirit of God descended upon them in all His fullness.

The blessing is also life - forevermore. There are several different ways of looking at this part of the Psalm. But we know for sure that "life – forevermore" is a blessing! It could mean that when we have adhered to the voice of the Lord and operated in unity; we will have life – forevermore. It could also mean that when there is unity among God's people, we ourselves will enjoy life in the truest sense, both now and forevermore.

The opposite of unity is division, and division can cause envy, strife, jealousy, confusion and every evil work to exist. When this happens to a body of believers, you will not find the blessings of the Lord there.

So far, I have talked about the four main points of blessings in Psalm 133, but I believe when God commands the blessings, they include every kind of blessing imaginable. Imagine angels standing in heaven with baskets of commanded blessings ready to be given out to all those operating in unity. Imagine them standing with these baskets but with nowhere to disburse the blessings. Or, maybe, they are just able to give out a few on occasions here and there.

How long has the Lord's prayer for unity in John 17 gone unanswered? How long will He continue to wait upon His Body, the church, to say yes to His will and His ways so the commanded blessing can be released upon us? The only unanswered prayer of Jesus is also the only prayer the Church can answer.

Chapter 7

Unity in Your Family and Home

Having unity in your family and home is one of the greatest things you can have. Every family should strive for this, fight for it, be determined to have it, and settle for nothing less.

My husband, Elisha E. Campbell, passed away on January 5, 2008, after 36 years of marriage. For the most part, our marriage was good. There was a determination to war in the spirit for unity, peace and love in our home. We definitely hit some bumps in the road, but we were determined that we were going to overcome and continue in love for one another.

God has always wanted unity between male and female since the beginning of creation. We see this clearly in the following scriptures taken from **Genesis 2: 18-24**:

"And the Lord God said, 'It is not good that man should be alone; I will make him a helper comparable to him.' Out of the ground the Lord God formed every beast of the field and every bird of the air, and brought them to Adam to see what he would call them. And whatever Adam called each living creature, that was its name. So Adam gave names to all cattle, to the birds of the air, and to every beast of the field. But for Adam there was not found a helper comparable to him. And the Lord God caused a deep sleep to fall on Adam, and he slept; and He took one of his ribs, and closed up the flesh in its place. The rib which the Lord God had taken from man He made into a woman, and He brought her to the man. And Adam said: 'This is now bone of my bones and flesh of my flesh; she shall be called Woman, because she was taken out of Man.' Therefore a man shall leave his father and mother and be joined to his wife, and they shall become one flesh."

These verses of scripture are basically dealing with the husband and wife in unity and becoming one flesh. God took the woman out of the side of the man's body, and this is where she is to remain throughout their union together. While it is true that the man is the head of the household and family, the two shall walk together, agreeably, as one, subduing and taking dominion in the earth. The only sure way of keeping Satan out of the home, out of the marriage, and out of the family is that the two, husband and wife, walk together in agreement. The power of agreement has great value and promises in it.

Matthew 18:19: "Again I say to you that if two of you agree on earth concerning anything that they ask, it will be done for them by My Father in heaven." This verse of scripture is referring to the agreement in prayer, but it is also very necessary that the husband and wife agree on other important topics, such as money matters and disciplining the children. While these two topics are important, there are other topics that are important as well. Any big decisions, that are to be made, need to be agreed upon by the husband and wife. It's also good to include the children when applicable.

Forgiveness plays a very important role in unity in the home and family. When we choose to walk in unforgiveness, we open the door to many attacks from the enemy.

Mark 11: 25-26: "And whenever you stand praying, if you have anything against anyone, forgive him, that your Father in heaven may also forgive you your trespasses." "But if you do not forgive, neither will your Father in heaven forgive your trespasses." **I Peter 3:7:** "Likewise you husbands, dwell with them with understanding, giving honor to the wife, as to the weaker vessel, and as being heirs together of the grace of life, that your prayers may not be hindered."

These verses of scripture are crucial to you getting your prayers answered. All of us are in need of forgiveness from our heavenly Father, and in order for us to receive His forgiveness, we MUST forgive others. What is said about the husband giving honor to the wife so that his prayers will not be hindered; I believe works in the same way for the wife. The wife must give honor to the husband also. This will cause them to dwell together in unity, getting their prayers answered.

Unforgiveness will not only hinder your prayers, but it will also cause you to live in bondage; a slave to the one you are not willing to forgive. Unforgiveness can cause pain and sickness to manifest in your body as you carry the burden of unforgiveness in your heart. I encourage you to forgive, because forgiveness frees YOU up!

Good communication is a must if you want to have unity in your home and family. There must be good communication between a husband and wife and good communication with the children. Even if something has happened to cause you to be angry; realize that's okay, but you must get it out in the open and talk about it. The word of God tells us in **Ephesians 4: 26-27:** "Be angry and do not sin." "Do not let the sun go down on your wrath, nor give place to the devil."

We sin when we lash out at the other person who made us angry, and when we choose to not talk about it at all. We must be willing to openly discuss what it is that made us angry, in the right way. We need to pray and ask God to help us, with that, by choosing the right words to say. Also, ask God to prepare the other person's heart to receive what you have to say, as well as you receiving what they have to say. When we refuse to communicate our feelings of anger and not allow the Holy Spirit to help us resolve the problem, we give place to the devil. This allows Satan to come in and magnify the problem by feeding all kinds of thoughts into our minds.

In the early years of my marriage, I foolishly would not talk to my husband when he did something to upset me. I would even go two or three days without talking to him; thinking I was punishing him. When he would ask me what was wrong, I would say "Nothing is wrong, or you know what's wrong." He would say "No, I don't know what's wrong, or whatever it is, I guess it's my fault." I praise God for His saving grace, mercy and love extended toward me during those times. I also thank Him for opening my eyes to His word, and for realizing it was pride that caused me to not want to communicate.

Satan knows the power of unity and oneness. That's why from the very beginning, he immediately set out to destroy the unity that Adam and Eve had. He wanted to destroy the plan God had for mankind. That's the same thing he wants to do to you and me today. He wants to destroy the plan God has for our lives by causing division in our homes and in our families.

Prayer is vitality important in keeping unity in the home. I really do believe the cliché' that says "A family who prays together, stays together."

There is a price to be paid, if we want to live in unity as a family. We cannot be victorious overcomers where unity is not present. It just won't happen any other way. You may see spurts of victorious living, but not long term without unity. Included in the price of unity will be giving up your right to be right. We do not have to always prove that we are right, and we do not have to always voice our opinion. Be willing to lay aside what you think and follow diligently after the spirit of unity.

Chapter 8

Teamwork

*I*f you are on a team of any kind; you must have unity in order to have a good team. You may be on a team at work, or you may be on a team in an outreach ministry or on a team at your church. You may be on a sports team or any other team that you can imagine; yet, there must be unity if you're going to be successful.

If you are a Christian, you should want to show your Christian values and Christian characteristics on your team. If you're on a team at work, or a sports team, you may be thinking, "I can't show my Christian values and characteristics on those teams," but "YES" you can. This doesn't mean you have to carry your Bible around with you all the time or that you need to demand to be given the opportunity to pray out loud. What it does mean is that you can show Christ-like love for your fellow teammates. You can encourage other teammates to work together. Where there may be discord; you can bring peace into the situation, especially by choosing not to participate in the discord. There are many, many ways you can let the love and the light of Jesus shine through you, and others will notice the difference. They will notice that your character and values are different. They will notice the peace that you have and some will even want what you have. Others may even ask why you act differently, and that will be your opportunity to tell them who you are and Who you represent.

You have to make a decision about who you will follow. Will you follow the opinions of others? Will you follow the world's view on what a team should look like, or will you follow Jesus' example? When we look at Jesus' team, we find that He transformed the lives of 12 ordinary and unlikely people to serve on a team. This team was not without problems, but their work created a movement that continues to affect the course of world history over 2,000 years later.

We all have influence, and our goal should be to have a positive influence that will impact the lives of everyone God allows us to come in contact with. On a team, we should always be looking toward advancing. If it's ministry, we should be advancing the Kingdom of God. On all teams, you should be working toward advancing the team, by building up and promoting each other to be all they can be.

I have served on many teams, both in ministry and in the workplace. My experience is that teamwork is a challenge, but it can, most definitely, be achieved. I worked with a team of ministers in a church setting, and there were times when we had our differences, as some of us were very opinionated, but we always kept unity on the team. Even though we believed what we believed, we did not allow those differences to come between us nor hinder the work of the Spirit of God. We realized it was not about us, but it was about pleasing God. It was all for the glory of God.

I have served on several leadership teams in Aglow International Ministries. My last position before becoming State Prayer Coordinator for the State of North Carolina, was serving as an Area President on a team in Virginia. It was a wonderful experience, as we were determined to settle for no less than complete unity on the team. When I think back, I believe we were able to accomplish unity, in such a great way, because we all knew that not one of us was as smart as all of us together.

When we are on a team, we need to realize that we're not only there just to serve the company, the church, the ministry, etc. We are also there to serve each other. In order to do that, we must put our trust in God. **Proverbs 3: 5-6** says; "Trust in the Lord with all your heart, and lean not on your own understanding; in all your ways acknowledge Him, and He shall direct your paths." We must give Him free reign in our relationships and in all our daily actions. His characteristics are to be applied to every aspect of our lives. We can be assured that if it worked for Jesus; it will work for us.

Never bring anything negative to the team, and never let our goal be to be served, but to serve. If our driving motivations are self-promotion and self-protection; we will use those to influence others to fulfill or meet our own needs. If our actions are driven by service and dedication to a cause that will influence others in a positive way, to build relationships, then we will model and encourage those values in others and build a better team. In **Matthew 20: 25-28,** Jesus' words to His team were: "You know that the rulers of the Gentiles lord it over them, and those who are great exercise authority over them. Yet it shall not be so among you; but whoever desires to become great among you, let him be your servant. And whoever desires to be first among you, let him be your slave – just as the Son of Man did not come to be served, but to serve, and to give His life a ransom for many."

Do you think these same principles Jesus demonstrated would work for us today, in a different culture, a different time, or a fast paced and high tech society? It would indeed. Jesus is the same, yesterday, today and forever, and so is His word. His word will never pass away. It is as effective today, when we apply it, as it was over 2,000 years ago.

A good team member will not get stuck in doing things the old way, but they will be adaptable and non-resistant to change. Remember when Peter and his fellow fishermen had fished all night and caught nothing (**Luke 5: 1-11**) and Jesus came along and told Peter to launch out into the deep and let down his nets for a catch. Peter's first response was "Master we have toiled all night and caught nothing; nevertheless at Your word I will let down the net." (It was like Peter was saying "We're the professionals here; we know what we're doing!") "But when they had done this, they caught a great number of fish and their net was breaking." In essence, Peter was astonished at what happened. He had to call to others to bring their boat to help them. Peter had only let down one net. He did not let down the nets as Jesus had instructed him. Imagine the fish they could have caught if Peter had let down the nets, instead of just one net.

When we are given a suggestion from a fellow teammate, let's not be quick to give a negative response, such as, "That will never work." Be willing to talk it through, as a team. Weigh the pros and cons and, above all, pray and seek God together whenever possible. It could mean a tremendous thrust ahead for your team into something bigger than you've ever imagined. True success is the fulfillment of the plan God has for you.

For unity to prevail on your team, you are going to have to trust one another. Without trust, it will be impossible for you to work together effectively. Trust is absolutely essential. I know you've heard the saying "You have to earn trust." I do believe this is, basically, true. Each team member has to prove him or herself trustworthy. When we trust people, it puts us in a vulnerable position, a transparent position, but also a caring and committed position.

When a wrong is done, we need to be quick to repent, apologize, to reconcile, and restore, because if trust is ever polluted, it's going to take time to restore. We're, actually, going to have to rebuild that trust again with our fellow teammates. So let's be quick to make things right.

Jealousy has to be completely thrown out the window! There is simply no room for it. Be yourself, and exhibit the gifts God has given you. You should never want to be someone else, or covet another's gift. God made you unique, and He wants you to be the person He created you to be. There is not another person on earth with your DNA. You are special, and your team needs you. They need the you that God created you to be.

As in any relationship, you must keep the line of communication open. You will never get to truly know each other if you do not communicate. There may be times when you will need to communicate the truth to a fellow teammate in love. Your communication must be honest and open, and always in the spirit of love. When you have established a good line of communication, a line of trust and love, your teammate will accept and receive your honesty because they know your character and they know you are not trying to hurt them.

Last, but certainly not least, I would recommend that each person on the team read **I Corinthians 13** periodically. It will change your whole view on how to love and treat one another. This scripture will help build unity on any level at any time. It will help you take your eyes off of yourself and place them on loving and caring for others. **(I Corinthians 13:1-8a)**

About The Author

*G*wen Campbell is a licensed and ordained minister of the gospel, called to be an Apostle of Jesus Christ. She received her Minister's license in the year 2000, earned a Bachelor of Theology degree in 2005, from Christian Life School of Theology, and was ordained in 2005 and commissioned to be an Apostle in 2012.

Gwen's husband of 36 years, Elisha E. Campbell, passed away on January 5, 2008. Three years after his passing, after living in Lynchburg, VA for 43 years, Gwen moved to Durham, NC where she serves as State Prayer Coordinator for Aglow International Ministries. Gwen has been a part of Aglow for 28 years, serving in various roles of leadership for most of those years. Gwen accredits a great deal of her spiritual growth to the Aglow Ministry, for it is the vehicle God used to set her free, mature her and prepare her to step into her purpose.

In June 2012, the Lord gave her the name "Shekinah Glory Apostolic Ministry," as the ministry she operates under when she's not serving in Aglow. God gave her this name because she desires to see God's Shekinah Glory show up in every meeting. "The Glory of the LORD filled the Temple." (**Ezekiel 43:5**)

Gwen attends Destiny International Ministries in Raleigh, NC. In June 2014, God led her to come into covenant affiliation with No Nonsense Apostolic Alliance in Raleigh, under the leadership of Dr. Shirley R. Brown. This ministry is moving her further along into the purpose God has called her to.

Gwen loves teaching and preaching the gospel of Jesus Christ. Her passion is to see every person step into their true identity to fulfill the purpose to which they were called, and to see the Body of Christ walk in unity.

Gwen works for Durham Public Schools as an Instructional Assistant for Exceptional Children. She considers this job to be very rewarding, as this, too, is a type of ministry.

She has two daughters, two granddaughters and one great granddaughter, all residing in the Raleigh/Durham area of North Carolina. She also has a step son, a step daughter, two step granddaughters, a step grandson, and four step great grandsons, residing in Virginia.

To contact Gwen, email her at: gwenkc7@gmail.com
Phone: 434-845-7532, or 434-546-2472